WORD FOR WORD

My Stand-up Act, Verbatim

By Mike Donovan

THIS BOOK IS DEDICATED TO 'BOB THE ROOFER'

SET LIST

FROM BOSTON
NH SIGN
BOSTON BLINKER
CT- NEVADA
GARDEN STATE
WHIPS & COSELL
WAITERS
SPECIAL VISITORS
INFO OPERATORS
ANSWER OWN PHONE
KRAFT MAC AND CHEESE
NINE MINUTES AGO
BROOKE SHIELDS
FAME
MICHELOB
PHONY BASTARDS
PEPSI SPIRIT
OLD MILWAUKEE
AETNA
SORRY
MNF DULL
SCULLY
FIND FACE

PIERSON
DEREK
SHEA
CHANDELIER
LITTLE LEAGUE
ROOKIE CARD
CRAPS
WE'RE 4
MY MOTTO
PC IDEA
TOP 300
FOOTBALL INJURY
HUGH MILLEN
DEADSLOW
PARCELLS
AMERICA'S CUP
ESPN CARDS
KOOL-AID SLOGAN
WHALER'S SONG
XFL
ERNEST SLOCUM
JUSTIN!
LOTTO ADS
12 FREE CDS
STEAK-UMM
PASSWORD
PROMOTE NEWSMEN

MATCH GAME

SANKA

BRIM

CHARLIE TUNA

QUEER EYE

FACTORY DAY 1

NEWLEYWED GAME

BARNEY

BEER

VERIZON JONES

BLINDWITNESS NEWS

OPEN MIKERS

SOX TRADE

BASEBALL TOO COMMERCIALIZED

RONALD MCDONALD

ALMOST FELL

SUGGESTIVE SELLING

BURGER KING

MOVIE HOST BOZOS

THE BIRDS

SILENCER

HEAVEN'S GATE

HEY QUEER

THAT GUY'S A QUEER

BOUNCERS

DRAGNET

AC SWEATSHIRTS

OSAMA BIN LADEN
FAMILY FEUD
WWWBLOMECOM
SOMETHING I LIKE
PHIL RIZZUTO
MOST PISTONS
STORE SLOGANS
KELLOGG IDAHO
MISTER ROGERS
FORK & SPOON
HUMPHREY
MOBILE VAN
DICK ALBERT
ARGUMENT WITH GAY GUY
QUAKER OATS
CLIFF
MIDAS
FLAKES AND NUTS
CHEERIOS
COFFEEMATE
CORN FLAKES
F.U.C.K.TED KOPPEL
299 BLANK
STARR +
THEY LOST
RIZUTTO/CARRY
THROW TO FIRST

TENNIS

DISTRACTING

GIBBS

STREET HUSTLERS

FROST

B KING – HERE'S SOME CUPS

HAVE TOLL READY

SUNSET

SIOUX CITY

TOM CLARK

MOOSE

BOGGS

HAVEN BROS

YOGI

CAPTAIN KELLY

COTTON SONG

TEAM PICTURE

PECK DEALER

REAL STORIES OF HP

COPS IN LONDON

WOUNDED KNEE

LEVITRA

DECOX

PECK AND CLINT

DOCTOR PHIL

ST. PATRICK'S DAY SONGS

HARRY THE DRUNK

PROFESSIONAL CHANGEMAKER
MY PILLOW
PRUNES
COFFEEMATE
BIG DRUG BUST
MERLE HAGGAGRD
POPEYE MASK
INDEX CARDS
HOCKEY
TABBY
RAY COMBS
TRUMP MACHINE
BOB DOLE
VEGOMATIC
HEROIN – XMAS
SHEA
KLAMOKLEX
COUSEY
SECOND SHOW
BLISS

Nice to be here, I'm from Boston myself. I can prove it:

"Hey, this place is pissa!"

Great to be here in New Hampshire. I like that sign when you cross the border: "Drive with courtesy – It's the New Hampshire Way"

They have a sign in the other direction: Drive like an ass hole! That's the Massachusetts way!"

If your blinker is broken in Boston, just use the Boston Blinker (arm out flashing middle f) "I'm taking a left, fuck you (crooked) sorry, a right.

Happy Ramadan! Nice to be here! Last week I worked in Connecticut, 'The Constitution State.' Now I'm in Nevada, 'The Prostitution State.'

I'm having a tough night. I got thrown out of the casino earlier. They caught me trying to jam Garden State Parkway tokens into the ten dollar slots.

I'd like to start off with a little impression for you, I hope you like it. If not ... it's back to Amway for me.

We take you back to the year 200, to the Adriatic Sea, to a Roman ship. My impression of a Roman slave being whipped in the galley ...

"Whoo whap! ..Uuugh – Whoo whap! .. Aaah – Whoo whap! .. Aaah!" All right it was too sick, I'm sorry. I went too far.

That bit goes over real big down in P-town ...

I try to go back to the material .. "No, just do the whips!" –All right, same pay, 35 minutes of whips. ... Except I get tailgated on the way home ...

All right, how bout someone that deserves a whipping. How bout Howard Cosell being whipped .. We should whip that fucker, let's face it ...

Howard Cosell being whipped:

"Whoo whap! .. Ow! The unbridled audacity! – Whoo whap! .. Ow! Unmitigated pain!"

Which is what that guy is, an unmitigated pain. You could walk into any barroom in America, on any Monday night, and hear some guy, leaning over his drink, and looking up at the TV and goin, "Howard, will you shut the fuck up?"

All over the world, for that matter. Guys sitting around little huts in Cambodia, "Howat! Shat ta fak uup!"

Guys picking it up on Jupiter, with giant brains, "How ow ow ard ed ed, Shut ut the fuck up up up."

It's because of those great insights he adds. What would we do without his tremendous gift for seeing things at a deeper level than us ordinary fans.

"All right, this is Frank Gifford, New England bringing the ball up. They're down by twelve, but trying to get back in the game here late in the third quarter.

Grogan pack to pass, he looks, he throws and .. it's intercepted! By Ted Hendricks at the forty, Hendricks still on his feet at the 50 and he is going to take it all the way in for the touchdown!"

"There! There! That's exactly .. what New England .. DID NOT WANT TO HAPPEN!" ...

No shit, Howard. ... They also don't like to stick their balls in trash compactors. Thanks for the insight, you toad.

Howard should be taken to Mount Saint Helens and be made to take the Nestea Plunge.

And no matter what player's name is mentioned, Howard's been there along the way. He always has a personal anecdote:

"All right this is Keith Jackson. Here's the pitch to Eddie Murray – pop – Hit's him in the head and knocks him down. But he gets up and goes to first base."

"You know something Keith, that's the way it's always been with Steady Eddie, I remember back in double-a ball, Abilene, the Texas League, they knocked him down there. But he got up, told me about it over ice cream that night. But they tried it again, Kokomo, triple-a ball, they knocked him down there, but he got up, told me about it that night. He always gets it up. I slept with him last night!"

Howard has a schitzoid personality. He's got two voices. First he's got the excited one: "GAME TWO OF THE WORD SERIES! YOU'RE HERE TO SEE IT WITH ABC SPORTS!"

Then he has the other identity. The tender Howard:

"The first base coach .. of the Kansas City Royals. WHAT a story .. of courage. He lost both his arms. He lost both his legs. BUT THERE HE IS! Being held up by members of his family, what a story of courage!"

The only story of courage is that Howard EVER shows his face in public.

But the more we hate him the more popular he gets. The only way you could really hurt him would be to have someone tell him off, right on the air. One of the other announcers, say, Keith Jackson. You'd have to get him drunk and talk him into it. "Come on Keith, you're the only one who can do it. You'll lose your job, but you'd be doing humanity a favor ... Get him a couple of whiskeys, he's thinking it over." Two hours later ... "All right, I'll do it!"

Next night you're watching the game:

"And it's another fine catch by George Hendrick!"

"You know something Keith, I had dinner the other night with George and he told me that .."

"SHUT THE FUCK HOWARD, WE HATE YOU, DIE IN YOUR SLEEP, YOU SUCK, YOU'RE A SCUM, EVERYONE HATES YOU! ... I'm sorry folks, I had to say it!"

Things aren't going too well back there; they've already beaten up two of the Chinese waiters.

We have some very special visitors here in the front row, there they are .. all the women I've ever satisfied. ... You laugh at that, you're cruel. I see we can work together.

No, actually it's the Ed King Fan Club.

I love working the Comedy Connection. It was recently voted best comedy club in the entire country .. by Comedy Connection Magazine.

Well, how are ya tonight, I'm in a good mood tonight, I made a few prank phone calls before I left my house, that always cheers me up. I just 'reach out and hurt someone.'

... I like to call the information operator; they deserve to be harassed as far as I'm concerned. They're always irritated with you cause you called them, you know?

"Information may I help you?" ...

What are you pissed about? I'm just calling you for some help, lady. ... So I give them a call.

"Ring ... Information may I help you?"

"Yeah, I'm a lazy son of a bitch, got the phone book right on the desk in front of me. ... But you know ... I'd rather let your fingers do the walking. ... Now listen, peon, get me this number and make it snappy. ...

Once in a while you get a male information operator. This throws me, I'm not used to it.

"Ring ... Hi, this is Ken, may I help you?"

"Yeah, blow me, can you give me the number of a uh Bob Johnson ...." Okay, I'm Sorry.

Here's a way you can answer your own phone at home, it throws people off.

"Ring … Hello is Bill there?" … A delayed reaction when you do it at home, too.

I hate the phone company. How many people don't believe in paying their phone bill until they get the final shut-off notice? … What the hell. You might die in the meantime, it would be wasted money.

The big thing on half the ads is that the kids aren't happy with the brand that Ma brought home.

"Maaa! This isn't KRAFT Macaroni and Cheese."

"Yes it is, in fact there's little K's right on the noodles there, you gotta look real close in order to see it … closer …. closer … How bout if I shove your fuckin face in there! … Nice n' hot too, right out of the oven. I work all day for a complaint, I don't think so. We'll have Jonestown Macaroni and Cheese tomorrow night, see if you like that any better."

Jonestown Food Products, with their world-famous slogan: "You'll never taste anything like it again."

I like to smoke the bones, that's my big thing, I'm not into the other drugs, personally, ah … someone laughs that knows me, heh heh. … Yeah, I smoke them once in a while .. like about NINE MINUTES ago …

I don't even like to ride the Mass Pike cause I don't like bones interrupted by toll booths. … You know, you're riding along, "Ah, shit, a toll booth, we gotta put the bone out."

Actually, you don't have to. The attendant is just as bummed out that <u>you</u> showed up, "Ah fuck, a car, I gotta put this bone out." Ya never know.

…

Every time someone dies from a hard drug they step up the anti-marijuana campaign. They're not finding a lot of dead bodies with half smoked joints hanging out of the side of their mouths … Let's differentiate a little here. … It's so ridiculous. Everyone's telling me not to smoke grass on these commercials. Brooke Shields telling me not to smoke grass? Oh, you're my mentor, I'll do as you say, Brooke. …

"Whatever you put in your body, will show on the outside." You must eat a lot of plastic fuckin sandwiches then. ... She shouldn't moralize with anyone, if she hadn't played a prostitute at the age of 11, she'd be answering a phone for Sears right about now. ... Fuck my way to the top and then condemn fucking. ... Bend over honey, I'll blow this next hit up your ass ... But anyway ...

The cast of Fame telling me not to smoke grass, guys with pink shorts, showing me their crotch: "Hey man, don't smoke grass." ... If you say so, hero. I never miss Fame.

"Hey Mike, wanna watch the Bruins game?" – "No, Fame is on. ... This is the one where Danny doesn't get the ad for the deodorant and everyone cries." ...

The whole cast of Fame could roll off a cliff in a fiery bus and I'd laugh my ass off.

... All right, maybe I wouldn't laugh, but I wouldn't help them. ... "Call for help." – "Couldn't hear ya, sorry."

They have a dumb slogan at the end: "You Can't Fly if Your High!" No. That's why you smoke the shit. What kind of logic is that? That's like saying, "You Can't Stagger if You're Drunk!"

Here's another one I saw … for Michelob. First of all their ads are sickening: "Weak minds were made for Michelob."

Then you got the: "Would two guys really go at it this hard just for a beer? They would if it was a Michelob Light!" Then they show these two guys, you know, one of them's trimming his lawn in the middle of suburbia somewhere, ya know. The other one comes over, "Hey, play ya one on one basketball."

"Naw no, it's too fuckin hot. I'm not interested."

"Hey … for a Michelob Light?"

"Huh … YEAAAAH!" …

As a matter of fact, Paul Barclay said to me before the show, "Mike, I know you're not feelin too good tonight, you've been having a lot of personal problems, but you know, please go up and make em laugh." And I goes, "Paul … I don't know if I can do it." And he says, "For a Michelob Light?"

"GIMME THAT MICROPHONE! HEY! GOOD EVENING LADIES AND GENTLEMEN, HEEEYY!"

What kills me is — Didn't it ever occur to these guys that they don't have to sweat it out in a basketball .. I mean if they really want a Michelob Light that bad they can go down the store and fucking BUY one, you know? ... These advertisers, they never considered that maybe if the guy loves Michelob Light that much, he might just happen to have some of his OWN in the refrigerator, you know? He's got a fancy upper middle class house and he can't afford a fucking Michelob Light, you know?

The other guy, "Hey FREE BEER! JEEZUZ! Michelob Light! Let's play hard, yaaa! Sweat, yaaa!"

Then you got these others, the so-called high-class beers, too. "Here's to good friends. A bunch of phony bastards" ... I hate everyone that's ever been on any of these commercials. Anyone that instinctually despises anyone that's ever been on any of those commercials, would probably get along very well with me, thank you. Sickening human beings, they should not be allowed to live, it's that simple. ...

Don't you watch certain advertisements and you say, "Whoever wrote that ad should be shot." Could you see me coming down to their house, "You're under arrest – blam! – That's for that Pepsi Spirit ad, you wrote it, I know it was you."

Old Milwaukee? Tastes as great as its name?

Must taste like shit! ... I see a photograph of Milwaukee, I don't get thirsty, okay? ... It doesn't make sense.

Oh yeah, it's a great ad, it has these five guys camping in the wilderness, it's three o'clock in the morning, they have the tent, the campfire, they hold up the beers and they sum it up: "Guys. It doesn't get any better than this!"

How bout a fuckin woman for openers, gentlemen ... These guys are gonna be porkin raccoons and they're telling me 'It doesn't get any better than this'? – If you say so buddy. – Guys are wiping their ass with leaves, 'It doesn't get any better than this.' ... To each his own. In the meantime I'm in my air conditioned apartment, a bag of bones, a VHS recorder, a woman blowing me, what a loser I am! ... Stop right now honey, I gotta go be with the guys.

Then you got these dumb slogans too: "Aetna, I'm glad I Metya"- Oh yeah, that's real fuckin hilarious. Then they got the Oriental guy, "Itnaa, Glad I metyaaa!"

They got a new slogan, "Aetna, spike in your retina - pffft!" ... Coz gave me that joke.

I'm sorry ... no I'm not ... I'm glad I said it.

Howard Cosell is claiming that Monday Night Football is dull without him. Yeah, Germany's dull without Hitler too, Howard. ... Oh, I'm so bored now.

But I think the most irritating thing about the World Series was Vin Scully for seven nights. ... Vin Scully? Every time you read the paper in the morning, "Vin Scully is the greatest announcer that ever lived." He's a fuckin pinhead! ... Vin Scully? "The ball kangarood into the staaands!" No, it fuckin BOUNCED Vin..

"That's a half a dozen hits, that's a half a dozen strikeouts now."

"Hey Vin, what time is it?"

"Quarter of a dozen to half a dozen."

I'd like to see him half a dozen feet under.

Garagiola was all right! But Vin, man he was .. He made things up: "You know, they call the bullpen in Boston, 'Williamsburg.' "

No, you fuckin made that up, Vin. They call it the BULLPEN.

"And the call all year long has been Clemens and Boyd and fill the void." No you made that up, Vin, they never fuckin said that okay? ... They got Hurst in there too. It's not like these two guys and everyone else is hopeless.

They lose the World Series. We're pissed off enough and all of a sudden, "Hey Boston! Don't hang your head!" Okay, we'll fuckin hang you instead, Vin … from a lamppost in front of Jordan Marsh … and we'll hock lungers at you like they did to fuckin Mussolini … okay, an especially vicious joke, but I heard a few laughs.

"Find the face that wrote it! Kick it in! Kick it in! Kick it in! … Marry me Sue – aaawwee."

The NHL went on strike in 1994. It wiped out the entire season! I was so mad I refused to go to any games! I put my skate down.

I like Johnny Pierson, he's in between the periods, with that segment there, 'Pierson's Pointless?' No, 'Pierson's Pointers.'

I liked him better when he traveled with the team. He was on top of everything. He'd know what happened even before they'd show the replay. There'd be a goal, you look around, 'That was a goal? I don't know what happened there.'

"Well Fred, I think what happened there was the puck struck the earring of a woman in the stands, then it bounced off the official's whistle, then it ricocheted off the back of six different skates, and it slipped into the far corner!"

Then you go, 'Oh, John, you're out of your mind." ...

Then they show the replay.

'That's exactly what fuckin happened!'

Of course he had his double-standards, too. If it's a rough play against the Bruins: "Well, watch this replay, Fred. I'll tell ya, that Dale Hunter, he's a dirty hockey player. We don't need guys like him in the NHL. He's not even a tough guy, he's an ass hole, there's a difference you know." ...

But it's a different story, of course, if it's a Bruins guy doing the same thing: "Well watch this fine play Fred! Jay Miller swings his stick over Wilf Paemont's head. Paemont's down, he's unconscious. Miller's a <u>fine</u> young hockey player, Fred."

You have to go to Hartford, when the Bruins are playing in Hartford. That's a lot of fun, 600 Bruins fans scaring the shit out of 15,000 Whaler fans ... in their own stadium. It's a total humiliation. ... They're like wind-up Frankensteins. They let em loose through the lobby at the beginning of the night: "Here we come! Bruins! Hey pal, come here. You and your family, we gotta tell ya something .. No come here, it's important ... ... The Whalers blow! Ha ha .. ha ha ha."

"Hey, good one, Joe"

"Thanks a lot."

We like Derek. He's the best. You know, if you read the letters to the editor, you'd think it was 50-50, you know, in the Sunday Herald, but you know, really, 98% of the people love this guy.

He's all heart. A guy on the other team bleeding all over the ice:

"He took a dive Fred, he's fakin it." ...

A guy on the other team could die right on the ice, I could see it now, vicious check in the corner, guys goes down, they stop the game, trainer comes out, looks up at the camera, shakes his head ...

This has never happened before. No one knows what to say ... Finally, Derek breaks the ice ...

"Hey I'm glad he's dead, Fred, whaddaya want me to lie to ya? ... Hey I'da killed him myself if I'da only had the chance, let's be honest. When are they buryin him? Is it Friday? Probably, tonight's Wednesday, no game that night, let's go piss on his grave, I hated that guy. ... I've waited for this day. ..."

He's such a tough guy, and then he has the A.A. spirituality side he tries to blend. Doesn't always blend, Derek ya know?

"We almost had an incident here in between the second and third periods here at Buffalo.."

"Yeah, but I kept my cool Fred. Everything worked out. … But for the grace of God .. I'da bashed that guy's fuckin skull in."

The eternal optimist, too. It's great the way he's so optimistic, no matter what's going on.

"Bruins are down by six, three minutes left. Another score, it's seven nothing."

"Don't worry, Fred, we'll get that one back."

Doesn't matter, Derek, we love ya for hopin, but we we're all giving up out here.

I like the instant replay guy, not this new guy … if you really watch the Bruins, at all, you know this guy, Dave Shea by now. This guy sucks moose, don't he? … Dave Shea? Look, it's just a basic principle of sportscasting that you hire as an analyst, someone who played the game. How can someone without experience, analyze a game? You and I can do the same job this guy does. Dave Shea?

"Watch the replay, Fred, Peterson has it on his stick, he shoots the puck, it goes in the net, nice play. He's been making a lot of nice plays like that lately, Fred. Let's hope he keeps making those nice plays, because the more nice plays he makes, the more goals he's gonna get, and you know what that means, more wins for the Boston Bruins, I was talking to him the other night he said he hopes to play better real soon and that looks like what he's doing right now, Fred." – Shut the fuck up. ... He's got nothing to say and he insists on saying it.

I'm glad this place has opened up again. As you know, it was closed for six weeks when the chandelier fell on the front two tables and killed three people.

Don't tell anyone I said this but, "I don't give a fuck about Little League, okay? I don't even follow the minor leagues, let alone Little League. They got this guy, what's his name Frankie .. Frankie what's his name ... Frankie Flynn, he's like five times bigger than the rest of them so he hits home runs. His real name should be Frankie Stein. ... Last year they had Danny Alimonte, they found out he was too old .. and they barred him for life, from Little league. ... Oh, what a penalty! What's next, Bob Hope can't compete in the Olympics next year?

Who gives a fuck about Little League? I don't.

I'm sorry. Now everyone hates me.

What else, I collect the baseball cards, I found a 1968 Nolan Ryan rookie card in my attic last summer .. with a fuckin moustache I had drawn on it with a Bic pen! ... Wow, what else do we have here, a 65 Mickey Mantle .. with fart bubbles coming out the back of his ass ... He's smokin a cigar .. there's a button on his uniform that says 'Eat me.' ... I wonder how much it's worth now?

... I wish that was just a joke.

The commercials they always so everyone smiling, having such a great time, they're playing craps.

They should have a realistic commercial:

"Goddamn son of a bitch!" …

You should know better than to play a game named after excrement. … If you had any chance they'd call it 'cupcakes.'

I see all these We're 4 commercials and they're painting a peachy creamy world that doesn't exist.

They show the kids in Roxbury ... then they show the kids in Southie ...

It's not goin like that, guys. Whoever wrote that ad should take the Orange Line home tonight.

So I wrote my own version of that 'We're 4' commercial and it goes like this:

We're 4, the muggers at night
We're 4, the streets without light
We're 4, the Roxbury slums
And the winos and bums on Pine Street

We're 4, the sludge in the bay
We're 4, the traffic delays
We're 4, a pickpockets day,
On the MBTA at Park Street

We're 4, tourist trap Cape Cod
We're 4, old Harvard snobs
We love to get lost in
One-way streets around Boston, it's infuriating

We're 4, the arrogant punks
We're 4, the staggering drunks

We're 4, belligerent cops
And adults throwing rocks, in South Boston.

… I'm only kidding, I don't even hate them, I just know everyone else does so … fuck it. I know how to pick my targets. 'Kick em when they're down,' that's my motto!

Come on we've come full circle, loosen up, who gives a fuck? Take the PC and shove it. … That's my philosophy.

This is quite a place. It has a great reputation. It was recently voted one of the top 300 Chinese restaurants in all of Ispwich.

I'm a football fan too, I love football, except when there's an injury, that sucks. Not cause you're thinking 'the poor guy,' you're thinking one thing only, "GET HIM OFF THE FIELD, NOW!"

That should have trap doors under the field, with chutes and slides. Woosh, Get him outa here. We'll read about your sorry ass in the paper tomorrow. Right now, we got a game to play, let's move it.

It's been a tough year to be a Patriots fan. It's been one HughMillination after another.

I like our quarterback, Drew Deadslow. Come on, I scramble for more yards in my living room than he does on Sunday. Zero is better than minus eleven.

Don't you hate it when he makes a bad play, and then they go to a commercial and he's trying to sell you something? Bad timing bro.

"Bledsoe back to pass, he's hit, the ball's loose, and it's picked up by an Oakland defenseman and he's going to take it all the way in for the touchdown. We'll be back, after this message.

"Hi, I'm Drew Bledsoe. Buy a Ford truck."

Fuck you, I'll buy a Chevy. I'll do the opposite of whatever you tell me to do .. because right now .. we fuckin hate you.

Talk to us next week when you're winning maybe.

Bill Parcells, there's a tough guy. Imagine him as your hone-room teacher in high school?

"Ah, Mister Parcells, can I use the boys' room?"

"WHAT THE HELL KIND OF A QUESTION IS THAT! YOU'RE A JERK! GO PISS IN YOUR PANTS!"

The only person who ever intimidated the media.

I don't follow all the sports, though. Who's got the time, there's 900 sports. You wouldn't have a life if you followed everything. The America's Cup?

Every once in a while you run into some Australian that's all excited cause they have it at that time.

"Hey Yank, we have the America's Cup now."

"Good, keep it forever. Who gives a shit? I wouldn't recognize it if you dropped it off on my fuckin desk. Bunch of millionaires go for a boat ride. Yeah, that's a sport.

Come on, how aristocratic can you get? Why don't you have a caviar-throwing contest while you're at it. Have the Bentley 500.

I'm gonna be at the next America's Cup though, I bought a PT-boat from a government auction. ... I'm working on it in my back yard. I all four torpedoes working right now ... As soon as I fix the 50-caliber machine guns it's anchors away!

I can see the play-by-play for that one.

"Here we are at the America' Cup now, Chester Chillingsworth the Third in the lead by a thousand meters, it's a beautiful sunny day .. And look at

that! Some maniac in a PT boat is attacking the
vessels! .. He's launching torpedoes! Surely this is
a joke … BOOM BOOM … It's not! .. Good God!
Some lunatic in a Red Sox cap has blown four
boats out of the water."

Leave a little not in a bottle: "Fuck the Cup."

That ought-a cheer them up.

What else? … Course I pick on it, but it is a sport,
I'll give it that much. Sometimes nowadays, the
stuff on TV they're supposed to be sports, they're
not sports. You turn on ESPN now – with all due
respect to the card players – you turn on ESPN
they show a bunch of guys playing poker … What
the hell is that?

Why don't they show a bunch of guys taking a
shit while they're at it, call that a sport.

"The ESPN Logrolling Contest!

Brought to you by Raisin Bran! Keep it rollin with
Raisin Bran!

McMurtry's taking the early lead – grunt –
splash."

Come on, that's not a sport.

... the Jonestown reference ... "Kool-Aid, You Loved it as a Kid. You Trusted it at Jonestown."

... Heh heh .. Isn't that beautiful? It happened 24 years ago and we're still fucking laughing about it.

"Drink the potion" "Yeah okay ya."

Every time the Whalers get a goal, this stupid theme song comes blaring over the PA: "Ba baa baa baa, bum ba bum pah baa, bum ba bum bum pa pa paaa."

"Excuse me sir, what's going on?"

"Oh, every time we get a goal, this theme song comes on."

"Well get rid of it, it's fuckin stupid."

You're better now, you don't need the theme song anymore. Originally, the song had lyrics:

"We're in last place, and we're losing again,

but at least we got a fuckin goal."

... Get rid of the theme song. It doesn't look good.

I feel guilty though, I drive down to Hartford to see a game, cause I don't feel like dealing with the Boston Garden. It gets a little rowdy, I feel mellow, ya know. I drive down there, ya know, it's more of a family crowd.

I get there, I'm watching the game, I get hit in the head with a hot dog.

"These Whaler fans are ass holes too!"

I turn around. Four guys with Bruins shirts:

"Bruins, yaah! ... We drive down to Hartford intimidate people, yaaah. ... It's a lot of fun for us, yaah."

You see them in the lobby before the game, ya know, a guy's walking by with his family:

"Hey, Whalers suck. How's that pal?"

I'm a football fan too. The XFL started up tonight, boy ... Triple XFL is more like it. Nothing but sex and violence, they had Whitey Bulger singing the national Anthem. ... Seka was singing back-up vocals.

"Boob boob boom. This session of district court will now come to order. is Mister Berger would you like to make an opening statement?"

"Yes I would your honor! The defendant, Mister Robert P. Scoutly, did on the afternoon of October third ... PUT A SLUG IN A GUMBALL MACHINE! .. A premediated crime for which the court must make him pay.

To allow this scum to walk the streets, would be a miscarriage of justice. I recommend life!"

"Mister Mason, do you wish to make an opening statement?"

"No, your honor. I .. <u>know</u> who's going to win."

"Very well then, Mister Berger will you please call your first witness."

"The prosecution calls, Mister Earnest P. Slocum."

"Yuswetellhotoonobutoosohelgod?" – "I do" "Sit down."

"Now Mister Slocum you are the owner of Slocum's Department Store, are you not?"

"Ye ye yes I I ..."

"Objection your honor, we can't hear the little worm."

"Sustained."

"Speak up ya little worm we can't hear ya!"

There probably wasn't a discipline problem in the OJ Simpson house.

"Justin! Turn that TV off!"

"But Dad!"

"Don't make me take my knife out!"

These lottery ads: "Have you played your number today?"

"Yeah, my family hasn't eaten in a fuckin week."

I'm in a good mood tonight though, I got my 12 free CDs in the mail today, where you join the club for a penny? ... They'll never see the rest of that fuckin money. ... How the hell do these people stay in business? – I've built a library on nineteen cents. ... Open up that mailbox ... "Su-kaas!"

And now, Jack Klugman for Steak-umm:

"Hey! Know what the best thing about Steak-umm is? When I don't wanna eat em, I steak um up my ass!"

I used to always want to hear a swear on Password.

"The Password is shithead."

"All right, let's go to the clues."

"Richard Nixon."

"Shithead."

"You got it. Ding ding ding ding!"

They promote these newsmen like I care who reads me the news. It's one o'clock in the afternoon: "Don't forget, tonight at 11, Tom Ellis!"

Oh wow, let me shit my pants. I was gonna try and get laid tonight, but let me set the alarm so I don't miss Tom Ellis. Like we're arguing about this at home, "I think we should watch Jack Williams" – "No! Tom Ellis is much better." I don't care if a fuckin armadillo reads me the news, I just want to find out what's going on.

Tom Ellis, I don't trust him. That guy could get into a fuckin tornado and his hair wouldn't move.

You know, they might as well have swearing on some of these game show, The Match Game? Are you kiddin me? They might as well run a porno movie instead.

Every question: "Mary said to Bob, 'Show me your blank.' "

Then the whole crowd goes, "Oooohhh." What the hell are they oooohin about, we're out of the seventh grade. If I ever got on that show .. or if they were ever stupid enough to let me on that show:

"Mary said to Bob, 'Show me your blank' – Mike"

"Ah yeah Gene, I think I'm gonna go with 'cock.' ... Hey, what are you mad at me for, Rayburn, what the hell else do you think she'd want to see? ... If you didn't want the answer, why'd ya ask? ... Hey I hear you blow Charles Nelson Reilly, is that true? Hey, I didn't say it was true, I just said I heard it."

How bout this guy, Robert Young, for Sanka. This guy laughs at nothing at the end of every ad.

"Feeling any better today?"

"Yes I am, Bob, now that I've tried Sanka."

"Ha ha ha ha ha!"

"Where's the fucking joke!"

How bout this, they got another commercial with the same problem. Brim decaffeinated coffee. What are these women laughing at?

"Fill it to the rim.."

"With Brim!"

"Ah ha ha ha ha ha ha!"

Where's the fuckin jooooke! What are these people laughing at, you know? I'm gonna coin that and mail it off to Reader's Digest, see if they like it down at the Laughter is the Best Medicine Department. If they use it, I'll make 50 bucks. I can see them reading it down there, ya know?:

"What's this? ... 'Fill it to the rim ... with Brim'? ... ... What the fuck is this supposed to mean?"

It's not even a bad joke, it's just not a joke.

How bout Charlie the Tuna? There's a dumb ad. Why the fuck does this fish want to commit suicide?

"Sorry, Charlie! You don't get your head your head ripped off my a meat-hook today!"

"Ah shit, I'm bummed out now. I wanna die!"

How do they know he didn't taste good, like they could look through the water, "He wouldn't taste good. Don't let that guy with the hat and the sunglasses into the net."

If he didn't taste good, they would just cut him up slowly and work him in with the good batches, and you wouldn't even know he was around. … You know that one black piece you always get in the can? That's Charlie.

"Sorry Charlie, nothing goes to waste in this factory."

I watched some TV today I saw that stupid show, 'The Queer Eye for the Straight Guy' – I'm developing my own show in reverse .. I'm developing my own show in reverse, it's called 'Don't Be a Wussy, Try Some Pussy.'

… We're trying to convert some of them back!

That's called 'working it off' in factory talk. I did a year and a half sentence in a factory, I know what it's like.

If it's your first day on the job in a factory, and you want everyone to like ya, there's an easy way to do it. All you gotta do is walk up to everyone, "Hey, you know what? The boss is an ass hole."

"Hey! This new guy's all right!"

I watch the Game Show Network, they have all the oldies, the Newlywed Game, with the sound-proof booth. "Okay wives, you know your husbands has been secluded off stage in a sound-proof booth. Isn't that right fellas" "Right Bob!" – Okay wives ..."

What a dickweed that guy is, huh? Bob Eubanks? He makes Wink Martindale seem hip. He is a dickweed. ..

That's one of my favorite words. .. I'm not making this up, in my neighborhood last week there was a sign on the supermarket billboard, the little .. whatever you .. bulletin board. They're looking for a lead singer:

"WANTED, LEAD SINGER. We're an established band. We have paid gigs. We have management. We like Def Leopard, U-2" and at the end "No dickweeds!"

Who's that gonna deter? Like anyone KNOWS they're a dickweed. ... Like some guy's gonna walking down the street: "Hey! I'm a lead singer!

Hey, management, this is great, I can't wait to call these .. U-2, they're my favorite ...Oh, No Dickweeds, I can't go. .. I'm a dickweed."

No one can know they're a dickweed. In fact having no idea that you're a dickweed is an integral part of being one. If you knew you were a dickweed you wouldn't be one.

How bout Barney the Dinosaur

"I hate you,
You hate me.
We're a dysfunctional family.
With a nick-knack paddywack,
Roll another bone,
My old man is always stoned.

Bees bother me. Bees, insects, bees. I mean every time you turn around, someone's telling ya how wonderful they are. "Mike, bees pollinate, we need the honey." Hey bees can sting ya in the scrotum when you're making loved in the

outdoors. They're not an asset in anyone's life. ..
But wait .. but what really gets to me is that every
time a bee lands on ya, ya always have some
chowderhead friend, "Hey man don't move. Just
let the bee walk all over you man, and eventually
he'll fly away."

Yeah, great advice. I've never been stung once
by a bee, and I only have one way of dealing with
them:

"A FUCKIN BEEEEEEE!"

You just swat em so far down the road they don't
remember who did it when they come back to get
ya. Some old woman in the background "Ow!" –
Heh heh heh heh heh.

Everyone's afraid of bees. Clint Eastwood, he
kills nine people: Click "Go ahead. Make my …. A
BEEE!"

I heard Verizon laid off 30,000 workers this week. Yeah ... They all got a call from James Earl Jones.

"You're no longer welcome at Verizon."

And now this Blindwitness news-note of community interest for you. The Massachusetts School for the Deaf will hold a two-week course in musical appreciation ... to be held outdoors at Logan Airport, and the public is invited.

… Something that's only bothering me apparently - Wait till these open-mikers get up here if you think I suck. …

It's great, you grow up getting beat up every day, you know, these little sick jokes don't bother you.

These are great times for baseball fans. If you're a Red Sox fan these are real happy times, huh?

Whoooa. Good times, I found out the Red Sox made another trade today. They made another trade. They .. they traded Jim Rice and Carl Yastrzemski to the St. Louis Cardinals for Stan Papi and a catcher's mitt. ... And they got the better of the deal. Stan is a big powerful hitter.

Baseball's too commercialized now, don't you think? You turn on the TV:

"All right, in case you're just tuning in, the Mets are down to their final two Maxwell House outs here in the bottom half of the Pringles ninth inning. They've scored two Rolaids runs and they have a Texaco baserunner on first.

Johnson looks in, gets the Chevrolet sign. Goes to the Heiniken stretch … now the Pepsi pitch!

Crack!

There's a Sears ground ball to short-stop, the Pizza-Hut flip to second, the Valvoline toss to first and it's a Home Depot double play!

So, the final score from Preparation H Stadium, it's the Minute Maid Marlins six and the Metamucil Mets five. We'll be back with the Reynolds Wrap wrap up; but first, a word from our sponsors!"

Ronald McDonald, a real Mcfunny fuckin clown huh? Wouldn't you like to be the guy with the honor of shoving a roman candle up that clown's ass? Come on.

You could smoke nine bones and he still wouldn't be fuckin funny.

If I saw five kids beating that clown up outside this building, I wouldn't step in to help ... except help the kids! It'd be like "Wow, where's that 2 by 4, spread his legs boys, right in the mcnuggets .. Bang!"

"Think he's mcdead?"

"No, I saw him mcmove."

[shot]

"Nice mcshot Joe, let's go find the Hamburglar and light him on fire."

Okay, that's a sick one.

Most comedy's cruel, let's face it. No one ever laughed because someone ALMOST slipped and fell on the sidewalk. The laughter only begins when that back hits the fuckin pavement.

McDonalds, they always ask you for something you didn't order anyway:

"Would like a pie with that?"

"Noooo!" Gets to be a royal pain in the ass.

But I found out, it's not their fault. I did penance there a few years ago, I did an actual two-month sentence as an employee at McDonald's. It was a rough time.

I was leaving little hints that I was not a happy employee, like I would take a bite out of the Big Mac before I put it in the box … The ground-glass McMuffin was the last straw … That old woman sure was bleeding when she came up for more salt. …Oh don't get bummed out, I didn't really fuckin do this, Jezuzz. "Oh wow, he's an ass hole, let's leave, oh … These are jokes, I write these at night.

How bout Burger King, 'Have it Your Way.' I got sick of that slogan I said, "I think I will." I went down there "Yeah I'll have a Whopper, a Whopper with cheese, large Coke, large fries, big bag, grabbed it, headed right for the door.."

"Where ya goin?"

"I'm having it my way: I'm not paying!"

That's their old slogan, their new slogan: 'Burger King, You Got it!'

Yeah, the runs.

Actually they should call themselves 'Burger Cold,' try getting a hot fresh one on the highway.

I can't stand these movie hosts. They give you too much information about the actors, it's distracting. I don't want to know if this guy went to Harvard in 1936, I'm trying to imagine he's a friggin' sea captain in 1812. You're ruining the movie for me, ya know?

Like Channel 5, the Great Entertainment, the guy comes out:

"Hello, I'm Frank Imadouche. ... Did you know, the star of our feature film tonight, in real life was known as a true scumbag? Yes, he beat his only wife, and raped his only son. In 1964, two suicide attempts ended in failure, much to the dismay of all of Hollywood. In 1970 he was finally beaten to death by a gang of angry people, each of whom he knew well personally. .. And now, back to .. The Life of Christ!"

Thanks a lot, Frank. You ruined the movie for me.

I saw a scary movie the other night, The Birds? Alfred Hitchcock? Boy what a scary movie. I've never forget the first time I saw that movie, I went right home and strangled my parakeet.

"What the fuck did I do?"

"You're one of them … crunch"

I felt bad later but … too late for Butch.

I do have a parakeet named Butch, I've only taught him how to say a few things:

"Fuck off!"

"Humans must die!"

"Birds are great!"

Here's something I want to know. This doesn't make sense to me. It's a scientific mystery. Why is it, like in a crime drama, like a 007 type movie, whenever someone gets shot with a loud gun, they scream in pain. "Pow!" "Aaaagh!" – But, if they're shot with a silencer "Pchum."

... I don't get it. How does that work? Someone give me the metaphysical explanation on that one. These people really cooperate with the script.

We'll have Jonestown Macaroni and Cheese tomorrow night ... ... Any crowd that laughs at Jonestown is all right with me. That was some funny shit in my book. I love those suicide cults. ..

Like the Heaven's Gate? Remember that? Is there anyone in here that did not laugh their ass off at some point during that one? I know I did. I was having a tough month, that cheered me right up. ... I wish I was jokin ... How stupid can you get?

"Here's the plan fellas: Cut off your balls, kill yourself, and then join me on a space ship."

"Okay, sounds good! Where do I sign? This guy's great!"

... Fuck it, start more cults. We can use the parking spaces ... That's what I say ... If you fell for that guy, you SHOULD die. ... Come on, what a dink. ... Yeah, his name was Doe ... yeah it was short for dildo. Come on, how can you fall for that dickweed, I dunno.

Here's something weird I know you always hear, you go to a comedy show you're bound to hear a couple of gay jokes in the course of the evening, but this is something that really happens, it's not like something I made up. Guys, this happens to ya, especially on the weekends, especially at night in the city. You're walking down all by yourself, minding your own business, and all of a sudden a car full of guys will ride by and roll down the window and yell at you,

"Hey QUEEER!!"

Isn't there a contradiction there, nine guys in a Volkswagen calling me a queer? ... I'm on my way to Sally's house to get blown, I don't know about these guys. ...

They're sitting on each others' laps and I'm a fuckin queer right? ... I dunno .. sorry I don't see any women in that car. ...

Then you meet these other people, these homo paranoid people, they really take it to extremes, "Hey that guy's a fuckin queer!"

"Well what'd he do Joe?"

"He looked at my shoe, he's a fuckin queer!"

I picture these guys having nightmares "I can't sleep, there's queers around!" ... Don't worry about it, Harry, it's not that important.

Then there's the other one for the truck driving school: "Tired of your dull job? Want to get into something exciting and glamorous? .. New England Tractor Trailer Training School is looking for you!" ...

They have them for everything. They have them for stewardesses, they have them for models.

But what about bouncers? I found out, I did some research into the matter and I found out that bouncers do indeed go to training schools, and it's located in South Boston .. and ah, .. and their commercial comes on at 3:30 in the morning on Channel 56, and ah, it goes like this:

"Aright .. dirty, filthy creep .. come on .. get out .. geet out! GET OOOUT! –" whoosh

"Hi! .. Have you ever been thrown out of a night club and said to yourself, boy, that's the job for me!... Have you ever wondered how much training it would take for you to enter the exciting and glamorous world of bouncing?

You man ask, how can I qualify for this highly professionalized field. Well, you'd be surprised how little training it takes to cross that golden fence, and become the bouncer instead of the bouncee. ...

Mass Masculine School of Bouncing, located right across the street from the Mad Hatter, will show you in just five long excruciating weeks how to become a professional bouncer.

You'll work in our simulated night clubs, just like ones you'll be bouncing in once you graduate. Specially trained loud-mouth drunks will start fights, spill drinks, insult women, and throw up, just like in real life! ... And it will be up to YOU to bounce them out!

Now let's look at a proud moment in the life of every bouncer. Graduation Day at the Mass Masculine School of Bouncing:

" ... Proud graduates ... today is the day you've all been kicking each other's face for. ... We've come a long way since that first lesson when we taught you how to ask them to leave, politely. Soon you'll be out in the clubs, and you'll have the world under your heel. And now it gives me great pleasure to present our trophy, the Silver Shoe, for highest final grade, to Mister John Byrne, John congratulations .. …uumm …uuggh … uummph …aggh ..”

"So why wait? In just five long weeks, you too can be a bouncer. And Mass Masculine is approved for veterans … boy is it EVER approved for veterans. … Call now, one of our representatives will stop by and demonstrate the training you will receive, by bouncing you and your family out of your own home!"

"Call now, our bouncers are standing by."

"The story you are about to see is true. The names were changed .. because we couldn't pronounce them.

This .. is the city. Los Angeles California. A lot of people live here. And a lot of them cause trouble. That's where I come in. I carry a badge.

On August 12, trial was held in the inferior court of Los Angeles. In a moment, the results of that trial.

The charges against the defendant were dropped because the judge had tried some of Bill Gannon's prune juice, and was in a hurry to wrap it up."

Great to be here in AC, where else can you find a guy from Bangladesh selling God Bless America sweatshirts, made in China?

God Bless America fine, God bless all peaceloving nations, how's that?

What's a turban and a pair of sandals walking down the street?

Osama bin Laden with the shit beat out of him.

If they catch him they should lock him in a room and make him listen to the Back Street Boys for the rest of his life.

How bout Richard Dawson, the Family Feud? Come on, if you locked him in a room with a rat, for five minutes, he'd fuck the rat, no question in my mind. ... This guy gets more cheap feels in one show than most of us get in a year and a half. He's not getting enough at home, that's all there is to it. ...

You only watch the show .. no one <u>watches</u> the fam .. You're not talking to someone: "Excuse me Joe, I gotta run. The Feud's on in ten minutes." ... No one watches the show. It's only on by accident in your house cause it's a busy time of the day, you throw the TV on, they take the surveys. "Hello? Am I watching TV? Well sort of. What am I watching, hold on a second ... aahh the fuckin Family Feud." - So it looks like one of every three families is really watching it.

You only watch, by accident, just long enough to get irritated with how stupid the people are on the show. At least me. You're watching it by accident ... I ah ... They asked this woman last week, "Name an animal with large eyes." She goes – budoodoop – "A beaver."

I'm sittin there at home, "You stupid fuckin idiot, lady!"

What the hell am I getting so mad about? I don't even know these people. Three o'clock in the morning you can't sleep. Hop into your car, drive to Los Angeles at a hundred miles an hour. Track her down, with a pictureof an owl: "WHAT THE FUCK IS THE MATTER WITH YOU, LADY!"

And what kind of an idiot do you have to be to get on that show in the first place:

"Name something you eat with a spoon"

(Whispering) "Ah yeah Richard I think we're gonna go with soup."

"Sooooouup!!! – Well that's a good answer! … Let's go to the board! Something you eat with a spoon! She said soup! … Survey said! …"

BUZZZZZ!

"Well I guess that was a <u>stupid</u> answer then, wasn't it!"

Now let's go to the Mongoloid Family! Hello there, lovely dear, stop bobbin your head so I can give you a kiss. … Everyone gets a wet kiss and a feel on the ass on the Family Feud! I'm a cheap pervert and an old friend of Bob Crane's. – All right dear give me a little kiss – little wet one bleblablu – look down the cleavage, NOT BAD! – Now let me straighten out my boner here and ask you this question. 'Something you eat with a spoon' - and don't give his answer like a stupid moron."

"Ahh ... soup!"

"TRY AGAIN!!! That was his answer!"

"Ah .. ah... French Fries" ...

"Now let me get this straight! Something you eat with a spoon and you say FRENCH FRIES!!! --- Well then I guess it was a greasy spoon she uses – Get it? A joke for everything! I'm so fuckin funny! --- Something you eat with a spoon! ... She said French Fries! ... Survey said ..."

Ding ding ding!

"Ninety-seven! ... Well I guess the Mongoloids brought their stinkin families to fill out the surveys tonight ... THEY DID! Look at em all out there in the audience bobbin their heads."

If you don't like anything in my act, you can respond at double-u double-u double-u dot fuckin blow me, dot com.

And my yamika came off.

All right … let me talk about something I like … … can't think of anything.

Half these announcers they have no idea there's a game going on. They're just shootin the shit for three hours while all the pitches go by in the background.

The worst of all time was Phil Rizzuto the Yankees announcer:

"You know I was having orange juice this morning in my hotel room, I gotta tell ya about this, White, there's a home run to win the game, AND I LOOK DOWN IN THE ORANGE JUICE …"

Phil there's a game going on!

Phil Rizzutto him and his commercials, "I'm Phil Rizzutto, the money whore!" …

But this guy, Johnny Most, when it comes to being objective, he was 'Johnny Least.'

"All right let's get a seat for this one, Johnny Most high above courtside ready to start the fourth quarter here at the Silverdome in Detroit. I'd rather be square-dancing in a leper colony! I can't stand it here! The fans here, this is a zoo, these fans, they're animals, these punks behind me keep kicking me in the head with their shoes ... They won't provide a security officer I asked for one an hour ago .. ow! .. Hold on a second ..

"I'll rip your eyes our of your fuckin face you little bastard! Come over here! I'll kill you right now!

"Ah .. we're having .. ah .. technical difficulties ... please stand by ..

"I have a gun right here, you wanna see it? Hey, I'll use it, at my age a life sentence is like ninety days. ...

All right Boston's trailing by six, 98 to 92, and they'd be winning this game if it weren't for these human vibrators they call officials. Jake O'Donnell and Jack Madden, you know, if you mailed away for a vibrator you'd get O'Donnell at your front door. There'd be a knock at the door and there he'd be, 'Hey you send for a dildo? Here I am.' ...

"You know something John, I'd like to point out a few statistics from the third quarter."

"I'd like to point out that in four years, you've never pointed anything out – smack! ... Just stay out of this – I don't need your echo tonight.

All right Bird inbounds the ball, in it comes to DJ, DJ fiddles and diddles, now he daddles, now he doodles, gets it down low now to Kevin, getting .. Kevin is getting kicked in the groin by Lambeer. And Jake O'Donnell just STANDS THERE AND WATCHES IT!

All right back up top now it comes to Bird, Larry stops, takes the pop, it's no-good, rebound .. all right we have a foul, I assume it's on the Celtics, everything else has been against the Celtics ... why should this be any different? Yeah, they're calling a foul on DJ THERE WAS NOBODY NEAR HIM! Who did he foul Jake, a spirit from another life? ... There wasn't a player within ten feet of him, you know? He must have caught Shirley McLain with an elbow as she floated by from 1870."

"Well John, I think what happened there .."

"I think you don't fuckin know what happened there Glen ... You're a bullshit artist from a talk show - slap! ... Just shut the fuck up. ...

All right, Thomas bringing the ball up, on the left over to Dumars, down low now to Rodman, back up top now to Th .. now something falls out of Parish's shorts, it looks like a nickel bag of marijuana ... It's getting kicked around the court, we have a time-out here, they're trying to slap a technical on Robert for having reefer on his person. But he's claiming it's not his. Course I saw it fall out .. wait a minute, I'm a Celtic loya .. I didn't see anything! ... Fortunately, Butch Hobson's at the game, he grabs the bag and heads out of the building ... He's gonna smoke it up with Bill Walton after the game. ...

All right Thomas inbounds the ball down low now to Du .. and it's stolen by Ainge, on the left over to Larry. Larry stops, he pops .. BANG! And he got fouled on the play! Arrrite! Well it's about time they called something the Celtics way, and Larry will go to the line and try to make it a three .. What? Nooooo! They're taking the basket away! They're calling an offensive foul against DJ I'm gonna kill Jake O'Donnell. ... I'm gonna kill him from the balcony." ...

"Well John, calm down."

"You shut the fuck up ... smack."

"I'm at least gonna yell at him. ... HEY JAKE! JAKE! LOOK UP HERE, IT'S ME, JOHNNY ... YOOOUUU SUCK! YEAH, YOUR MOTHA. ... Hey they can't call technical on the announcer, I can yell anything I want.

All right, Thomas bringing the ball up. Thomas .. Now Laimbeer pulls a knife out of his trousers! ... And he stabs Larry Bird right in the ass! ... AND THEY'RE CALLING THE FOUL ON BIRD! ...

It's always Laimbeer, I hate that bastard. You thought I hated Kareem? That was nothin, I'd rather blow Kareem than shake hands with Laimbeer. ... I hate that guy! He came up to me before the game, he said, 'Johnny, Johnny, it's my last season, why don't we bury the hatchet.' I said, 'Good idea Bill! In the back of your fuckin head!"

...

Well listen, I had a nice time, thanks a lot.

"Sears! It's the fun place to shoplift!"

"Lechmere! Where you pickpocket the difference!"

"Radio Shack, you've got questions, we've got hassles."

"I-Hop, Come in hungry, leave without paying!"

I got a ride from this truck driver. He took me from Kellogg, Idaho to Morgantown, West Virginia. And he gave me a lot of words of wisdom, I was a more impressionable young man at the time. And the one thing he stressed most often I'd like to share with you now, because I carry these words of wisdom with me to this very day:

"You know Mike, you gotta go for the ugly girls. They're the ones that fuck!"

… 'Thanks, thanks Champ. Thanks for the advice. … Words I'll try and live by.'

Course they have some good shows on public television. Sesame Street, the greatest kids show of all time.

And Mister Rogers, that was a good show too, the late Mister Rogers, poor man, he's moved on to a better neighborhood. … He was a weirdo in my books, I don't care what anyone says. Who would want their son heavily influenced by that dude?

"Let's go look at Picture Picture, see if he has any messages for us today. … You're special people to me. Because I have no friends in the real world. In fact, my life's going down the drain ... But you can't go down the drain ... You can never go down, can never go down, can never go down the drain .... I'm a generally fucked up individual ... Hello Picture Picture. Any messages for us today? ... Mister Rogers took it up the .. Take the cameras away from Picture Picture! That's not true! I'd never do that with a rhino! .. I guess Picture Picture's not in a good mood today. Let's see if the trolley will take us to the Neighborhood of Make-Believe .. where it's ridiculously obvious that I'm doing all the puppet voices."

I found out about him, it was in his obituary, believe it or not, he was in the Marines. Can you imagine that? Imagine getting your ass kicked by him, you'd have to kill yourself! You'd be on the George Washington Bridge:

"Hey buddy don't jump. What could be so bad?"

"Mister Rogers beat the shit out of me."

"Down ya go! .... Looosaa! .. splash!"

Like that photographer that got slapped by Richard Simmons. Turn in your dick right now buddy. There's another loosaa. Midwest 'loser. That guy's a loser.' Around here, 'looosaaa.'

True story about the Boston accent I swear to God, I'm a believer, I swear, this really happened, my cousin was ten years old when she moved to California from South Boston. The second day in school out there she got suspended, cause she went up to the lunch lady and she said, "I need a faak and spoon." That really happened. I swear on the Bible, the Torah, the flag, the whole nine .. My aunt went down, tried to explain it, they didn't believe them, it's still on her record to this very day. ... Her recid. She got the faak an shaft.

I love that story. I know it's true cause she's still pissed off about it to this very day. If it was a bullshit story she'd laugh.

There's a Boston version of Hoarders, called Hoddas.

My next impression, Hubert Humphrey: "I'm just as pleased as punch that you asked me that question. But I'm not going to answer it."

You gotta give them credit where it's due though, 4 5 & 7, they each have a helicopter now, they give you video traffic reports live from the air, that's tremendous. If you have a Sony Watchman in your car, you can see yourself stuck in traffic. "Hey there I am! Hey I need a paint job, I didn't realize. Heh, let me give the finger to the guy next to me. Hey I can see that, all-right, heeey."

Now that's a good service. Sometimes though, you have these radio stations, they think they're gonna help you out in traffic with a 'mobile van.' Am I the only person this bothers, this is stupid, ya know:

"Now let's go to the WRKO Mobile Van, with Joe Smith."

"Joe Smith in the Mobile Van, I've been stuck in traffic for nine fuckin hours, I haven't moved. ... The guy in the blue Chevy might be jerkin off, I can't be sure. .. The guy on the left is smoking a pipe full of hash, I'm getting a contact high right about now. All I can tell ya is don't go to Watertown Square cuz I can't get outa here to save my life. Back to you."

Yeah, thanks for the report. Get a mobile pedestrian while you're at it, with a walkie-talkie. It'd do just as much good.

How bout ah Channel 2, public television, they make you feel … You're pissed at me. Why? She was laughing until you came back, and then you've been giving me a dirty look and now she's stopped laughing. What are you mad about? … All right … what else, how bout ah, public television, they make you feel guilty..

… Bunch of dopers out there, I didn't realize

How bout that show Evening Magazine with Barry Boring and Sarah Deadwood.

"Dick Albert, he brightens your day!" No, he makes me severely fuckin depressed.

Yeah, I'm two years' old. "Today's weather F & D! F & D! That's fine and dandy!"

No, that's faggy and doofy. It stands for foolish dickweed, okay?

Last week a big temperature drop, He's got the words BIG DIP on the board:

"Hey! We're looking at a big dip!"

What a coincidence! I was thinking the same thing!

Come on Dick, you're an idiot.

"Today's Albert Quiz. Dick Albert is a big dip, true or false? The answer is …. truuuue!"

You have to be careful if you get into an argument with a gay guy, cause you never know what you might say: "Oh yeah! Is that right! You know what you can do? You can SUCK MY FUCKIN … never mind. … Stop staring at me, it was a figure of speech.

"You said I could."

No I didn't. It wasn't literal. Stop staring at me.

They have a different perspective on things. A gay guy asked me last week, "Mike, how are the Red Sox looking these days?"

"They fuckin BLOW!"

"They must be a good team then."

They had another one for Quaker Oats, they're talking about the stupid guy on the box with the hat and the wig. The voice-over: "You've been waking up to his reassuring smile for a hundred years."

Reassuring?

Yeah, whenever I'm down in the dumps ... the Quaker Oats guy picks me right up. In fact I got out of bed the other day, "Ah shit I don't feel good. All these bills ..... Nothin's gonna cheer me up .... Heeey. The Quaker Outs guy! Why feel down when you have a friend? Come on buddy you and me, let's go out for a couple of beers."

What am I an ass hole?

The Old Man of the Mountain fell down, I was very sad.

He has a new name … 'Cliff!'

Everything has to have a slogan, right?

"Take it to Midas. Take it to someone you trust!"

Make up your mind. …

Hey, nobody trusts Midas … nobody.

How bout the cereal ads, they're pretty bad, for the same reason every time. The people get much too excited about the stuff. More than anyone in room would in ten lifetimes:

"Hmm … chomp … this is still crunchy in milk. … Look at this. Flakes and nuts and … gee, this is something special. What is it?"

It's cereal ass hole, keep your pants on! Don't give this guy a Santoro's meatball sub, he'll jump off a building.

They're all like that.

I saw this one for Cheerios, for example, the old man's about 50, the son's about 20, he's been away a couple of years I guess. He comes home, eats Cheerios, the old man flips:

"Since … when did you start eating Cheerios again?"

Here's a realistic response:

"Since when did … anyone give a fuck? … I don't even care, Dad. If I had just grabbed the Froot Loops, it wouldn't have made a bit of difference to me. You're senile, dude, no wonder I left home. … Since when did I start eating Cheerios again … since you lost your job."

"What was that, son?"

"Nothin. I didn't say anything."

I like to do my version of different ads. Remember this Coffeemate commercial, years ago, they had this guy headin up the cabin in the winter time? He'd be sharing the guy's place, he kicks in the door:

  "Boom … Nice place … Nice of Bob to let me use it for the weekend … Think I'll have some coffee .. uh, no cream, looks like I'll have to drink it black .. huh, what's this? Coffeemate non-dairy creamer. … Carnation makes it … must be good. …"

  What a bunch of shit. … I'd be imagining my version of that ad:

  "Boom … Nice place … What a sap he is to let ME use it for the weekend. … I don't like the guy. None of us do, we just use him. Heh heh ha ha. … tthwwack .. spit … Nice painting, heh ha ha … Think I'll call the time in Seattle and leave the phone off the hook … I'll rearrange the labels in his medicine cabinet, heh heh heh ... Now I'll take advantage of him and have some coffee. Cheap bastard, no cream! ... Yeah, what's this .. all right I'll try it .. Oh, Carnation makes it, must suck .. smash" .. Right through the window.

They have another one where the kids supposedly catch their parents eating THEIR Corn Flakes, get it?

"Dad, are you down there eating our Corn Flakes?"

"Oh gee, ya caught me now."

Then some stupid voice-over 'You loved them then, you still love them now."

How bout a realistic version:

"Dad, are you down there eating our Corn Flakes?"

"Yes! And I paid for this shit, now GO TO BED! ... Ungrateful bastards. ... I'll steal your pillows if I feel like it. ... I had a life, once."

The following is a public service announcement: "Give to the Fund for Underprivileged Children in Korea. Send your dollars to FUCK. 21 Bangme

Boulevard, Cummington Mass., 04169. This is your chance to show that you give a fuck,"

"Paid for by FUCK."

"Give to the Center for Underprivileged Nuns in Texas ... Send your dollars to ...

"We are experiencing technical difficulties, please stand by."

I like that show Nightline, but where did they get this guy, Ted fucking Koppel? ... I'm convinced that man was chased home from school every day as a child. "There's that faggot Koppel, get him!"

"Oh I'll make up for this, I'll be famous someday." Come on, he looks like Howdy Doody.

I sent away for that book James Coburn's always pitching on TV, 'How to Beat the Casinos.' I sent away, 300 pages, 299 blank, last page: "Stay the fuck home."

Come on, everything's X-rated nowadays. Did you read the Starr Report? I liked the part where he said he put his head under her dress .. but he didn't inhale. ... That was my favorite part. ..

I .. I keep hearing this one thing over and over: 'If only he'd been honest. .. We want him to be honest. .. Bill, just be honest.'

I don't think we really want that, do we?

"I want you to listen to me because I'm only gonna say this once: I .. love ..pussy ..."

I don't think we really want him to be that honest ...

"I don't care, I'd let Madeleine Albright sit on my face, I don't give a ... You want me to be honest, you got it." ...

He's gonna be the first president on a postage stamp with his fly open. ...

He has a lot of nerve naming his dog, 'Buddy.' What a stupid named for his dog, 'PUSSYHOUND's the only name for his fuckin dog! ... He's got the dog trained to find the hottest interns.

"Woof wo woo!"

"Good boy, Pussyhound. Nice goin!"

Grabbin her by the dress, "Raaagggh." ...

He's gonna be the only president with his presidential library at the back room of the Foxy Lady. ...

What's his memoirs gonna be titled? I read a lot of the presidents' memoirs. 'R.N.' was Richard Nixon's. Bill Clinton, 'B. J." ...

Oh .. a .. Gerald Ford, 'A Time to Heal.' Bill Clinton, 'A Time to Kneel.' ...

Did you see the Barbara Walters interview? She asked her about lifting her skirt. She said, "Well, that's part of flirting. It's a dance!"

..Yeah, it's the fuckin Bimbo Limbo ... the Charleston Chew ... the Knee Pad Polka ...

Don't feel bad for Monica, though. She just signed a big contract. She's gonna do some Milk Mustache advertisements ... Hey, I didn't say anything, you guys filled in the blanks on that one .. heh heh." ...

You gotta give them credit though, they're both patriotic. She was striking a blow for freedom and he was sticking up for his country ... Everything worked out. ...

Bill Clinton as a little boy: "I cannot tell a lie, Father. I chopped down every cherry in the neighborhood." ...

Of course most fans are only with the team when they're up.

"Hey, how'd they do this week?"

"They lost ... They suck."

"Hey, how'd they do THIS week?"

"We won, we're number one."

Oh, I see how it works.

Half the announcers have no idea there's a game going on. They're just shootin the shit for three hours. … They're just having a conversation while all the pitches go by, it's ridiculous.

The worst was Phil Rizzutto:

"You know, I was having orange juice this morning in my hotel, there's a home run to win the game, and I looked down in the orange juice and .." … Come on, Phil.

Harry Carry, the Cubs announcer, this guy was shitfaced before the game started:

"Hey! This Bud's for me! .. So's this one! And this one! And this one! … Sandburg up .. burp." …

They have another announcer, Duane Staats. That's supposedly his real name. Yeah, I'm fuckin Jack Funnybone. ..

Course baseball does get too slow, sometimes, that's a common complaint, I agree sometimes. When there's a guy on first, that drives me nuts. They throw over there about a hundred times! They should have a rule, if you don't get him on the second toss, he gets second base. You know? That would put an end to that horseshit. ... It goes on for twenty minutes.

"All right here's the stretch ... The throw to first, the runner's back."

"Come on!"

"All right, he goes to the belt, he gets the sign ... the throw to first, the runner's back."

"Jesus Christ.."

"Here's the stretch .. he steps off the rubber."

"Come on! Pitch the ball. We have jobs 'n shit."

It gets ridiculous. You wish the announcer would at least liven things up when that happened, it wouldn't hurt anybody, ya know.

"Jimmy Rollins at the plate ... Jimmy's hitting .262 with 26 runs batted in. The throw to first, the runner's back ... ... Jimmy likes to fuck chickens in the off-season. ... Hey, I'm only kidding, I don't know that about him. But I had to say something, goddammit. I could read War and Peace before this inning's over."

Tennis I don't follow. The only time tennis makes the news is when some idiot like John McEnroe, or one of his punk imitators, loses his temper at a line judge. That's news? Gimmie a break. He's always yelling at some little 70-year-old line judge in a 12-foot chair, what a tough guy:

"THE QUESTION, JERK! WHERE WAS THAT BALL? ANSWER MY <u>QUESTION</u>!"

Then he smashes the water cup around. Oooohh. ...

They should have Marvin Hagler as the line judge.

"That ball's out."

"HEEY! ... Good call."

"Thank you."

… have my family to think about.

I like to call up people for no reason at all, for example … … Hi … we're doing a show here .. I know I'm not that great, but I don't suck, give a chance will ya? … Yeah … Like I figure if it's in the middle of the night and I don't know what time it is, I lost my watch, I figure why call that cold, heartless recording from the phone company when you can get that same information from a human being … Look I warned you politely once, now SHUT THE FUCK UP! … It's distracting to me, you don't understand, you only have to listen to these jokes, I have to fucking remember them. There's like a LOT of them I have to try to keep track of.

"Oh."

What the hell are you talkin about?

For two years I though the name of that song was 'Gravity.'

You couldn't understand what they were saying [sic]

I like the way they sang in the old days much better. Barry Gibb would sing something like this: "It's … on..ly words … and words are all I ha…ve .. to .. take your heart ….. a…way..aaay."

And the other guy, Robin Gibb, would sing something like this: "I staaed a joek – weech staaed the ole weld cra-eeeng." And a little musical intro here" "Dee nuh nuh nun naa, dun ana nini nuna dina na nanaaa, I waak the oonee stree, I wat the pepal assing baii."

Come to think of it I didn't know what they were saying back then either. Didn't make any difference.

One more time for Glenn Jensen, did a great job, let's hear it for him! … All rightie.

Nice to be here, I've been up and down the strip today, everyone hustlin' ya, they wanna know where you're from. It's just a hustle:

"Hey! Where ya from?"

I finally snapped: "Where am I from? Get Out of My Face, Montana." …

The guy didn't miss a beat, he said: "That's a coincidence, I'm from Thanks For Being a Dick, Idaho."

"Hey! Where ya from?"

"The place where they give out the good jobs. You've never been there."

... a little Robert Frost to cheer them up. ...
Let's see ... who else do I hate?

They say, 'Have it Your Way,' and they're the only fast-food chain that makes you do all the work. Where do they figure with this slogan, you know you're on the turnpike, you got some friends with you, 'Hey wer'e in and outa here, you guys thirsty .. allright ... I'll have ah, two Cokes and a coffee."

"Here's some cups, the shit's over there!"

"Have it my way? My way is for you dickweeds to do this stuff for me. Charge me an extra dime, I don't care. This is rest stop, not a work stop. ... What's next, if I order a hamburger are you gonna hand me a machete, "The cow's in the back, dude." "Oh, have it my way .. I didn't realize that's what they meant."

I dunno, I don't like these toll roads, how bout this sign, like on the Tobin Bridge: 'Have Toll Ready.'

How bout kiss my Irish ass. Have your fuckin lips ready. Have toll ready., we'll wait till I get there and I'll search the floor for the fuckin nickels. Have toll ready, jump off the bridge, buddy.

I love doing this for a living, it's a great job getting up at the crack of sunset.

There was a famous plane crash in Sioux City Iowa, a jetliner in a ball of flame landed, and the .. the captain was a big hero – Captain Haynes as a matter of fact - cause as soon as the plane landed he jumped on the PA and clamed everyone down.

I'd like to recreate for you now that little announcement he must have made:

Pssht - "Gooood afternoon everybodee and welcome to Sioux City. Sorry about the rough landing … Temperature outside right now in Sioux City is about .. seven hundred and seventy degrees … and considering half of you are on fire, the captain has decided to lift the no-smoking ban … Enjoy the extra dry roasted nuts … For those of you who plan on dying, make sure your corpses are in a full upright position … and thanks for flying Ignited." … That's a sick one, I know.

Of course, Red Sox fans are the most loyal, you know that. You go to the game they're right behind their players, no matter what.

I went to a game last summer, Tony Clark wasn't having a good year, but the fans were right behind him when he came to bat.

"Come on Tony, you can do it baby!"

"Come on Tony! Just a base hit, brother!"

"Little ground ball to second."

"You fuckin SUUUCK!"

… Come on, you know it's like that. …

Yeah, the worst fans take all the credit if a team wins the whole thing. The drunks, they're down there at the celebration:

"Hey! We're number one!"

"Yeah, number one! Number one. Number ONE!"

No, THEY'RE number one, you're a useless fuckin dickweed pal. You could die tomorrow and no one on the team would know about it, let alone give a shit. … You're number six billion.

How bout the Patriots, it's like Christmas Eve, ya know? … I'm not gonna sleep tonight. At the crack of dawn I might take a nap, that's about it. .. If they win it's gonna be biggest victory in the history of Boston. It's gonna be unbelievable. .. If they lose it's gonna suck moose. ...

Did you see the Father's and Son's Game at Yankee Stadium this year? Wade Boggs showed up with 603 kids. I thought that was nice. He's a good shit.

Why pay 40 bucks for a closed circuit fight when for free I can stand in front of the Haven Brother's Diner and wait for the bars to close.
'Serving shitfaced alkies since 1878.'

"Hey Boo Boo! Do you smell what I smell?"

"... I sure do, Yogi."

"Hey look over there, Boo Boo. It's one of them long-hair type tourists .. and he's tokin on a Yogi-Stogie! ... Why don't we wait till he's gotta take a leak, then we make a dash with the stash, eh Boo Boo, nya ha heh hee!"

"Mister Narc wouldn't like it Yogi."

"What's gotten into you you leapin little pothead. Mister Narc is after them too. So if we get away, it's a-okay! Nya ha heh hee! ... Now's out chance Boo Boo! You make for the cave while I move with speed and grab the weed! Nya ha hey heee! .. psshhew!"

Meanwhile, in Narc Smith's office

"White Shoes Johnson says 'Arright!'"

… That kinda sick. I don't know how you people can laugh at that. That's really disgusting, you people should be ashamed of yourselves.

Okay, I'd rather come out and just do a sick joke, out and out, than do it with the subtlety that commercials do. I mean, did you ever see that commercial for Captain Kelly's smoke detector? Now what the smoke detector is, it's supposed to be an alarm to make sure that your house doesn't burn down, and everybody you know, everybody gets out in time. And they could just tell you that. But instead they dress this guy up in a fireman's uniform, with the little cap and everything.

And they have him stand in the foreground, and in the background is smoldering rubble. ... Now what is this supposed to mean? He never comes out and says what it's supposed to mean, but we know. Why doesn't he just come out:

"... Hi ... People that used to live here? ... They're dead. ... Dead! Corpses! ... Had to get a goddamn dentist to find out who they were. ... They ain't gonna see the light of tomorrow. They ain't gonna see the light of any day ... cause they're dead.

Don't you die. Get a Captain Kelly's Smoke Detector, today."

Combat was my favorite show. The two most important questions in life are 'What is reality; and why did Vic Morrow never run out of bullets? And why did the Germans always aim at Vic Morrow's heels?'

The worst commercial of all, my vote, singular category is the ah Cotton song:

"The touch the fee eel of co tton, The fabric of our li-i-i- ives."

What the hell's the matter with this ass hole? If you feel that sick, you shoulda stayed home pal.

Christ, the Bee Gees are laughing at this guy's singing. Not a good sign when …

He rammed an elbow into Parrish's nose so hard, he's gonna look a little different for the team picture next year. And they're calling the foul on Parrish!

Gregory Peck as a drug dealer:

"It's good shit, now give it a chance. It's creeper. You'll get baked if you give it time. This isn't fucking Sears and Roebucks, you can't return it. If you try and return it I'll have your fucking legs broken. If you don't like it you can flush it down the toilet. I'm not taking a loss for you. You've been sucking bones off me for three years. This is the first time you've actually tried to buy any. You're pushing your luck. You're an ass hole."

Actually, I don't smoke and drive, cause I'm too paranoid, cause I watch my favorite show all the time, "Real Stories of the Highway patrol!"

That's a cool show. They should have a realistic one though, just once. Maurey Hannigan comes out:

"Hello, tonight we'll ride with Ohio State Trooper Benny Sullivan, as he .. takes a bribe, drinks on the job, threatens his wife at gunpoint, and harasses a black motorist for no reason at all."

"These are the real stories of the Highway Patrol!"

Realistic ones, ya know?:

"Looks like I found some cocaine in the car, ma'am. Course if you blow me, I didn't."

"These are the <u>real</u> stories of the Highway Patrol!"

COPS is good but they don't have the ending for ya. Real Stories you at least know what happened at the end.

COPS is good, that was the original. They had COPS in London, two weeks ago, that was a good show. They had to change the theme song though:

"Bad blokes, bad blokes. What ya gonna do, what ya gonna do when the bloody bobbies come for you. Bad blokes, bad blokes."

... That's my version of that commercial ... Those Indians, they're getting us back for those bad treaties.

"You take em land, we take em pay check."

They will too, they'll clean you out. Why don't you put an arrow in my back on the way out the door while you're at it? ...

They should at least give you a bumper sticker if lose more than a thousand bucks: "I Got Scalped! ... At Mohegan Scum."

... They should have sound effects on the slot machines when you lose:

"Che shu ... Tough luck white man!

Che shu ... Sucks to be you, pale face.

Che shu ... That's for Wounded Knee, ass hole.

Che chu ... Tonto cool, Long Ranger dildo."

You have to set a limit to how much you can lose, and don't go over that limit, I'm pretty good about that. .. As soon as I've lost three year's salary, I walk away. I have my family to think about. .. I know when to say when.

And what's going on with this country? Every other commercial now is hard-on medicine. Slow it down, will ya? You try to watch the 6 o'clock news, there's 19 different brands competing for your boner, come on, slow it down. ... It started with Bob Dole, "Just because my arm hangs down helplessly, doesn't mean my dick has to. ... I'd much rather lose an election than an erection." ...

Ya, ya got the Levitra one, the older guy he's trying to throw the football through the hoop, he misses, symbolism, oh oh. Then he tries it again, pffft 'Right through! Ha haa! She's gonna get a dickin' tonight, yeaah!'

The wife comes out, winky winky, let's go inside, young stud.

Ok. That's a good analogy if you're a guy, 'Okay, my dick is a football, 12 inches long, big and fat, nice and bouncy, that's cool. ...

If you're a woman you should take offense,

'My pussy's a fucking tire swing? A 30-pound hunk of raw, dry rubber with a hole in the middle big enough to fire a Tomahawk Missile through, without scratching the sides? That's the best you can come up with for me? Put the writers back to work, get em a pad of paper and a laptop. Come up with something more charitable than that. Why don't they show a guy throwing a banana into the Grand Canyon while they're at it?

What if a guy's 20 years old and he starts taking that shit, what's gonna happen then? He's gonna be putting holes in fuckin brick walls. ... You'll recognize this dude. He'll be the one being arrested by six cops:

"I'll fuck ANYBODY! AAARAAAGHH!"

They're dragging him off to the decox.

Gregory Peck for Viagra: "It makes Moby Dick so hard, it could Kill a Mockingbird!"

Clint Eastwood for Viagra: "Go ahead, make my boner."

What else? I watched some TV today, oh I saw a few minutes of my hero, Doctor Phil. He's so insightful. He sees things on a deeper level than us ordinary people:

"So you're tellin me he's always drunk, he's never had a job, he slept with your mother, he slept with your sister, calls you a bitch and a whole every five minutes and he's put you in a hospital 11 times .. Maybe it's time you should start thinkin about no longer being with this person .." ...

Thanks for the insight, King Solomon. How much are they payin this ass hole, I coulda told her that."

Arright! Happy St. Patrick's Day! That was a real song, now a spoof of a famous Irish song:

"When Irish guys are fighting,
Sure it's like a long night-maare,
You can hear the bottles brakin,
You can see them pullin hair,
When Irish punks are shitfaced,
There's no reasoning with them,
And when Irish eyes are bloodshot,
They'll start fights with their own,
Best frieeeennnd!"

We interrupt this program to bring you this special news bulletin: Harry the Drunk is dead.

"Don't you have anything smaller? Don't you have anything smaller than this!"

"Yeah, my dick, will that do pal? ... No, I measured all the bills with a ruler. They're all the same size. ... I'll buy a piece of bubble gum with a 50 tomorrow, see if you like that any better."

Now that's bad enough, but a <u>toll</u> attendant, <u>they</u> get mad? The guy snaps at me last week, on the Mass Pike … "Is that all you got is a 20?!"

"Hey pal! .. You're a <u>professional change-maker</u>! You exist to do this! And nothing else! They have an exact change lane, I wouldn't be here if I didn't need this very kind of help! Why are you mad?"

That's like the post-man coming by, 'Here's your mail you pain in my ass you!' … 'What did I do?'

Same principle, you know? If you give them a 1 they're all right, "Here's your change, drive safe, have a nice day."

You give them a 20: "Sigh … … you fuckin piece of shit." They start slamming the money around, giving it back to you real slow .. Then they think they're gonna get back: "I'm gonna have to give ya back nineteen ones."

"Good! Then I won't have nineteen more ass like you pissed at me for the rest of the day. … Go back to that crossword you've been working on since the Anita Hill crisis. … Moron.

And after they drag his useless carcass out of there, put the fuckin Mypillow ass hole in his place.

"I couldn't sleep, I tried dozens of pillows!, I still couldn't sleep. Weeks went by, I tried 800 pillows, nothing worked, months went by, I was hallucinating.."

TRY JERKIN OFF YA FUCKIN WEIRDO!

I hate that fuckin guy! I'd like to murder him with his fuckin pillow.

"Ohh it's the best pillow ever! Double your money back you've never had a ... bett ....er ... pi...."

"Errrgh ... errrgh ... ugh ...."

"... You're right. It does provide a nice long sleep."

Let's put it this way, I would befriend the Jordan's Furniture guy, if he would help me beat the shit out of the Mypillow guy.

Then the three of us can go mess up Flo from Progressive. ... Everyone hates that bitch. We should all draw straws tonight, and whoever gets the short straw has to track her down and ice her!

... Where was I ... I digress.

I saw another ad for "Prunes! They're great for breakfast!"

Yeah, have 15 or 20. They'll appreciate it down at the office cubicle. Have a nice big bowl of chili while you're at it. Wash it down with some expresso. … Then go para-sailing in a kilt. …

"Hey, a convertible … boink … bull's-eye!"

Come on, I'm not proud of all these bits but that's fuckin funny.

"Hey, a convertible! .. Boink"

How bout the coffee ads, the people on the coffee ads, they open up the can in the morning, they flip out over the smell.

Whoosh. Inhale deep.

"Aaaaaahhh!"

Relax buddy, it's just coffee! There's only one smell that and no one's ever put it in a fuckin can.

...

Imagine if they did?

Snatchwell House!

Taster's Moist! ...

Fill it to the Rim ... With Trim

Skanka! Twice the poon-tang, half the caffeine!

Chock Full of Sluts!

Hills Mothers

A lotta guys are gonna be getting hard-ons in Starbucks tomorrow. "Hey what going on? Oh .. that stupid fuckin comedian."

I like the way they announce drug busts on the news:

"Big drug bust in Reno! Action News 8 will take you there!"

Sounds good to me, let's go. You never know what leftovers are lying around, what the hell.

Music for 200, the answer is ..

"Lead singer of Rolling Stones group, last name rhymes with Dagger."

Ding – "Chuck"

"Who is Merle Haggard?"

They're gonna have to come up with new field sobriety tests for pot smokers, cause they can walk the straight line and do the ABC's no problem, you know?

Cop breaks out a 67 cent Popeye mask, if you laugh, you're fuckin busted. ... He dangles a stale Twinkie ...

"You want that, don't ya?"

"No"

"Yes you do, here ya go ..."

 "Yes ..raaah"

 "Lock him up!"

I like the electric marquis next door, ya know, ya got

"Booze! Gambling! Strippers! Whores! .. Catholic mass, Sunday at ten.

Bad news about the Monopoly slot machines, apparently they were manufactured by McDonald's … yeah … no one's winning today … they have a new slogan, "You deserve the shaft today." They should give everyone a free hamburger for Chrissakes.

I wrote a TV ad for Smith and Wesson:

"Hey Donovan, you're a prick!"

Boom!

"Smith and Wesson! If you don't like what they say, BLOW THEM AWAY!"

I like the XFL, I don't mind it, some people hate it, you know I don't mind. They have a running back on the Las Vegas Outlaws, his name is "He Hate Me." You're allowed to have nicknames, it's in your uniform I think he ... He's injured now, I guess he's now called "He Hurt Me." You know, what's is gonna be like in a couple of years?

"Eat shit back to pass! He's going deep for Your Mother's a Slut! But it's intercepted, by Kiss My Black Ass! ... And coach Blow Me is furious! ... And we have an injured player on the field, it's 'Rotate On It.'

You know who they're aiming for from their commercials: "It's the XFL! Brought to you by, Trojan Condoms. If you've got the dick, we've got the raincoat! And by, Jack Daniels, because ... beer is for pussies!"

What else, the Boston Marathon? It goes right by my house, but I don't follow it too closely, I gotta admit. I just show up around five o'clock with my lounge chair, pop a couple of Genesees ... watch the last few stragglers come in" "Hey you suck buddy, give it up! Ha ha ha ha! ...

Ah shit, where's that bag of marbles? ...

I'm only kidding, I wouldn't do that, I'm out there helping out those tired runners with my cups of sour milk, just in case they're thirsty. ... I watch them do their Shemp impressions for me.

Even if they were gay, I wouldn't care. Elton John's my favorite singer and he's gay:

"Don't let your so-oon go down on meee."

"And I think I'm gonna suck a long long dick."

"Hooold me closer tiny hamster."

... You handled that well. Last week in Atlantic City a crowd booed for that joke. Come on, now let me get this straight, these guys put animals up their ass, I'm the bad guy for making a JOKE about it? ... I don't think so. That's cruelty to animals big time in my book. These are the only gerbels on earth going, 'Please! Put me in a test lab, will ya? Rub the shampoo in my eyes, I don't give a shit. Kill me! Just get me out of this guy's ass!" ... I'm against that. I'm a political comedian. I'm against people putting animals up their ass. I'm gonna write a letter to the New York Times about it tomorrow, see of they publish it. I'm selling bumper stickers after the show: 'Friends Don't Let Friends Put Animals Up Their Ass." I feel like adopting these poor gerbels, I feel bad for them. What would you name them. "Hey, Buster Brown, how are ya?"

I wanna see swearing on Who Wants to be a Millionaire:

"Are you gonna go for the $500,000, or you gonna be a fuckin pussy and stop right now? ..You're out of lifelines, ass hole."

I miss Pee Wee's Playhouse, that was a good show. I always thought they'd catch Mister Rogers first, but you never know.

He's a lefty, did you read that? ... It was in the story. ... I rented the movies he was watching, I figure they must have been great ... they cost this guy his career ... Nancy Nurse was one of them.

Man, that's quite a good review: "I whipped it out."

… I just show up around five o'clock with my lounge chair I watch the last few stragglers come in, 'Hey you suck buddy, give it up!' – [laugh -plus 'aww' & 'Booo!']

Oh fuckin boo I don't do this shit! I write these jokes down on index cards while I'm smokin bones at three in the morning what the fuck [cheer] What the fuck .. people editorializing. These are jokes, okay, it's a night club, you got the smoke comin up, it's all fuckin fiction, all right? [cheer] .. You gotta snap once in a while you can't take it ya know – This moral disapproval. That's why we do this for a living, we like being a little bit rebellious, okay? If we wanted to kiss your ass we'd be doing something else for a living [cheer] .. Just telling it like it is.

What else, I love hockey too, I love the announcers, they describe the fights depending on who wins.

If the home guy wins, "Oooh, Thompson pounded the shit out of him that time!" – If the guy on the other teams wins, "We don't need this kind of violence in the NHL."

If the other team's off sides, "The play is off sides."

If the home team's off sides, "The play is CALLED off sides. Tonight's official, Wally Harris, he lives at 36 Oak Street. ... Egg his house, he's an ass hole. ... Now's a good time to do it, he's at the game."

Yeah I confess, I admit it, I have experimented with marijuana … it was about three hours ago. … No, I don't defend the other drugs, but grass, come on, it's not good for you, but they're not finding dead bodies with half-smoke bones hanging out of the side of their mouths, lighten up, give us one drug for Chrissakes. We're not criminals we had a tough week we just want a fuckin buzz.

It's a natural instinct to want a buzz, that's why they sell catnip for cryin out loud … You're telling me Tabby can get stoned and I fuckin can't? … I don't think so. Me and the cat are getting baked together, tonight.

"Good shit, huh Tabby?" – "Meeeooow!"
"Leave those Rollos alone, those are mine, ass hole."
"Fuck you meeeow!"
I don't even have a cat, but you know what I mean.

You got that new guy Ray Combs, he whacks it, no one likes him, he doesn't count.

They have a line of talking slot machines ... there's a presidential series.
There's an Obama machine. It promises hope, it delivers small change.
There's a Trump slot machine. It's great. Even if you lose you can claim that you won.

There's a Biden machine, it doesn't remember how much money you put in.

I saw a Lincoln machine, I said hey I'll give it a shot.

How bout Bob Dole for erectile dysfunction.

Please Bob, I'm eating my dinner, okay? I don't wanna think about 90 year old guys with hard-ons right now, if you don't mind.

"Just because my arm hangs down helplessly, doesn't mean my dick has to. I lost the election, not the erection."

Remember Vego-matic? "Slices, dices, onions, vegetables, in seconds!" And the guys cuts his fingers off? Remember that? I always imagined if marijuana ever becomes legal, the same people that made Vego-matic will make a new product, and their ad will go something like this:

"Why spend hours cleaning that fresh new pound, when you can have Dope-o-Matic do it in seconds. Yes, with Dope-o-Matic you can clean pounds, ounces, nickels, or even mere handfuls of nature's finest.

Simply drop it into the miracle vacuum bowl and let Dope-o-Matic do the rest! Watch with glee as the twigs are separated from the batch and ground into a rollable smokable mixture. Imagine the crop you can have after Dope-o-Matic selects only the largest, ripest seeds, and drops them into the automatic Dope-o-Matic seed return slot.

This great new product usually sells for 6.5 billion dollars. But if you act now you can have Dope-o-Matic for just $7.77! Here's how to order!

"<u>Rush</u> $7.77 to Dope-o-Matic, box 116 High Street, Walla Walla Washington. … Be sure to include a joint to show your sincerity."

Well I have to get going soon I have a major heroin deal I have to complete.

… All right, you've been a wonderful crowd, thanks a lot, Merry Christmas!"

You got two guys in this town who never played the game and they made them analysts. It's a total hoax … Dave Shea? This guy's useless. I know as much as this guy.

"Well watch the replay, Fred. Middleton has it on his stick, he shoots the puck, it goes in the net, nice play. Let's watch it from another angle, there he is holding the puck, there he is looking at that goaltender, there he is shooting it, there it is in the net. Nice goal, ya know that's a big goal for the Bruins, they were down by two, now they're only down by one, let's hope they get one more goal and tie this thing up, who knows, maybe they'll take it into overtime and win this thing."

Shut the fuck up! You don't know anything and you never shut up. You whack it, pal.

And all these medical ads:

Do not take Klamoklex if you have a history of sudden death. Klamoklex is not recommended for anyone under the age of one, as some infants have reported having suicidal thoughts after taking Klamoxlex.

Bob Cousy's a great announcer, it's hard to say anything bad about a guy like him ... but I'll give it a shot. ... His diction leaves a little bit to be desired.

"Ah, Wick Wobey and Warry Bird went up for that webound."

... Who the hell is Wick Wobey? I don't see him on my pwogwam here.

Attention. Attention. We have a second show that is waiting to get in. So we hope you had a great time and we thank you for coming out to the Ding Ho, but please ... GET THE FUCK OUT!

There they are! The Ignorance is Bliss Club.

THE FUCKING END

www.ingramcontent.com/pod-product-compliance
Lightning Source LLC
Chambersburg PA
CBHW070343220526
45467CB00001B/237